I0471053

Book Law
for Authors

Mary Hutchings Reed &
David Creasey

LAWYERS FOR THE CREATIVE ARTS

CHICAGO, ILLINOIS

The materials contained in this book represent the opinions and views of the authors and/or the editors, and should not be considered the opinions or views of the law firms with the authors and/or editors are as sociated.

Nothing in this book should be considered as providing legal advice for a specific case, and readers of this book should obtain such legal advice from their own counsel. This book is intended for educational and informational purposes.

Book Editor: Jason Koransky

Book Designer: Patricia Rios

Library of Congress Cataloging-in-Publication Data
Reed, Mary Hutchings
Creasey, David
Book Law for Authors
Mary Hutchings Reed & David Creasey
Library of Congress Cataloging in-Publication Data is on File.

ISBN-13: 978-1490981024

ISBN-10: 1490981020

To order copies of this book, please contact:
Lawyers for the Creative Arts
213 Institute Place, Suite 403
Chicago, IL 60610
(312) 649-4111
info@law-arts.org
www.law-arts.org

Table of Contents

Introduction

In celebration of our 40th year of service to the arts, Lawyers for the Creative Arts ("LCA") decided to produce a series of books on various entertainment law related legal topics, LCA Law Guides.

LCA is proud to offer to our clients and the general public its first LCA Law Guide, *Book Law for Authors*. We believe that this book will assist you in your creative efforts and point out some legal issues you may face as an author. If you are able to recognize the issues before they become a problem, then we've done our job.

For more than 40 years, LCA has provided an invaluable service to artists. Today, this service is made possible through the dedicated work of the LCA staff, including our Executive Director, Bill Rattner, and our Legal Director, Marci Rolnik. We hope the LCA Law Guides will be a valuable aid in that effort.

My thanks to Mary Hutchings Reed and David Creasey as authors of this LCA Law Guide, Mary Hutchings Reed and Barry Irwin as the Chairs of the 40th Anniversary Committee responsible for spearheading the production of the LCA Law Guides, Jason Koransky as editor-in-chief of the series, the authors of the other LCA Law Guides, and the LCA Board of Directors for their continued support of this project.

To make sure that our efforts are in line with artists' needs, we welcome your input on the value this book has for you.

Jerry Glover
President, Board of Directors
Lawyers for the Creative Arts

About Lawyers for the Creative Arts

Since its founding in 1972, Lawyers for the Creative Arts ("LCA") has been the "go to" resource for legal advice crucial to the creative arts. Regardless of a client's ability to pay legal fees, LCA provides legal advice to individuals and organizations in the arts and entertainment communities directly and through our network of volunteer attorneys.

LCA serves individuals and organizations in all areas of the arts and entertainment, including the literary, visual, and performing arts. From string quartets to rock bands; from screenwriters to graphic designers; from costumers to sound engineers; from sketch artists to producers; from stage actors to street vendors; from bronze casters to photojournalists; from figure models to fashion designers; from theaters to circuses; from literary publishers to media houses; from museums to digital archivists; LCA helps them all navigate the complex legal system.

We have helped clients start businesses, draft contracts, and protect innovative designs and creations of every nature in every conceivable discipline of the arts. Through the Patricia Felch Arts Mediation Service, we have helped artists resolve disputes quickly, privately, and outside the costly realm of courtroom litigation. When necessary, we have also helped clients pursue lawsuits. Most of our clients are seeking to become financially successful. However, we also specialize in advising new and existing not-for-profit organizations, providing counsel from inception to dissolution. We have helped thousands of organizations, including many of the most prominent and successful arts organizations in the area.

LCA operates with a small full-time staff, but we are backed up by several hundred active volunteer attorneys from the best firms in the area. Our volunteer lawyers are the true heroes who level the playing field when clients are at a disadvantage. They are willing to step up and contribute their time and valuable expertise to our many thankful clients. They *get it*—that art, in all its forms, is an important and worthwhile piece of American culture, and that art and those who create it should have legal protection.

The long list of volunteer attorneys, together with LCA's dedicated staff, Board of Directors, and Honors Council, are the soul of LCA. With their support, artists are free to do what it is they do—bring color, texture, and wondrous sights and sounds to all of our lives.

To meet the ever increasing demand, we have grown our volunteer base over the years, enlisting thousands of attorneys, and we have networked to place matters in other states and, in fact, in other countries. In the past 12 months, LCA has provided critical legal services, in one form or another, to more than 2,000 individuals and organizations in all areas of the arts. Our phones and e-mail continue to buzz with artists who are in dire need of legal help.

We constantly hear praise from our client artists, entertainers, and writers for the volunteer attorneys who have helped them. Those attorneys make it possible for the artists to concentrate on delving deep into their hearts to produce the most provocative, most beautiful, and most audacious art they can find within themselves because someone else has taken care of their legal concerns.

Education is another key element of LCA. We provide materials, conduct workshops, and give seminars on not-for-profit incorporation and tax exemption, the law of music, publishing, film, copyright and more. We give presentations to dozens of schools, colleges, law groups, and arts groups each year. And, we mentor hundreds of young lawyers.

As we celebrate 40 years of service, we pledge to continue, with the help of the legal community and other supporters of the arts, to provide our unique, high-quality, and necessary services to the artists and arts organizations throughout Chicago and Illinois.

William E. Rattner
Executive Director
Lawyers for the Creative Arts

How to Engage a Lawyer

Whether you are an aspiring author ready to pour your heart and soul into your first work, regularly writing, or already braving comments and critique from an editor, it is important to slow down, step back, and remember to seek legal advice on the content of your work.

So when is the right time to consult a lawyer? The truth is that it is never too soon and that more often than not, a client will approach a lawyer well after mistakes are made that could expose the client to legal problems.

Lawyers for the Creative Arts ("LCA") has been conducting client outreach for the past 40 years in order to educate the public about legal issues and help artists like you to know not only when to reach out to a lawyer but also to know that pro bono and low-cost legal assistance is available.

LCA is one of roughly 30 Volunteer Lawyers for the Arts, or "VLA," organizations in the United States which offer free legal services to income-eligible applicants. To determine eligibility, an individual or business generally needs to submit a request for legal help and disclose the individual's gross annual household income and/or the gross annual revenue of the business. VLA staff attorneys will then conduct an intake meeting to assess the scope of legal work needed and follow up to seek pro bono (no legal fees) or low-cost legal assistance from a pool of willing volunteer attorneys.

If you are not in need of pro bono legal assistance, the best referral source is often from a fellow writer who has experience working with his/her own lawyer. You may want to ask around in writing circles and then do some homework online by checking the attorney's record.

Every state maintains an attorney registration and disciplinary website that provides public information on licensed attorneys. You should check to be sure the attorney you are considering is: (1) licensed to practice; (2) carries malpractice insurance; and (3) does not have a disciplinary record.

Although many states do not generally require lawyers to carry malpractice insurance, having it is an indicator that the lawyer is responsible in running his/her law practice. If you find past disciplinary complaints, weigh the information prudently and inquire with the attorney to obtain an explanation. The complaint may have been unwarranted and dismissed.

You can also find an attorney through your local or state bar association, as each generally maintains a referral program. For example, in Illinois you can search for legal counsel at illinoislawyerfinder.com, a service offered by the Illinois State Bar Association. In the Chicago area, you can obtain a referral from the Chicago Bar Association by calling (312) 554-2001.

Lawyers are also the best (and sometimes worst) critics of other lawyers. Reliable sources of information on the best lawyers in particular fields of practice include lists published by Leading Lawyers, Super Lawyers, and Martindale-Hubbell, which all award attorneys based on a peer to peer rating system.

Once you find the attorney who is right for you, the attorney will usually present you with a letter describing the scope of offered legal services along with information on the lawyer's legal fees. This is called an "engagement letter" and is customary in the legal profession.

The engagement letter serves as your contract with your lawyer. Attorneys write engagement letters often to signal the beginning of representation and to tell the client what to expect, including whether others at the law firm may work on the file and the way that fees are calculated.

If an attorney agrees to provide pro bono legal services, the attorney may still write an engagement letter for you to sign, indicating that all regular legal fees will be waived. Nonetheless, you, the client, are often responsible for any out-of-pocket costs, such as business filing or copyright or trademark registration fees charged by the government.

Artists able to pay an attorney often want to know how much legal fees should cost. Unfortunately, there is no easy answer to this question other than the age-old "it depends." This is an honest answer, as it is quite hard to predict how much time, for example, it may take an attorney to negotiate with someone on the other side of a contract or how time consuming a dispute may be.

That said, you can expect that an experienced attorney who has worked for ten or more years in a major metropolitan area likely charges several hundred dollars an hour or more and that attorneys in less populated areas with less experience often charge less. If an attorney works for a major law firm with multiple offices nationwide or globally, you may often notice his/her rates are also higher than an attorney in a mid-sized, small, or solo practice.

Attorneys in these smaller practices are more autonomous and generally have more flexibility to adjust their rates if they so choose by capping the number of hours spent, offering a fixed fee, charging a rate lower than their regular hourly rate, or charging a deferred fee such as payment that comes out of a publisher's advance to a writer. You should discuss these options carefully and make sure that you understand the fee calculation so there are no surprises at the end of the day. Remember that you are never bound to any one lawyer and can terminate the attorney-client relationship at any point in time and ask for a copy of your file.

If problems ever arise, try to communicate the issue to the attorney and recognize that attorneys are often juggling many legal problems for a range of clients all at once. The attorney may need to read over his/her notes from your file prior to taking a call, so be as patient as you can be when working with your lawyer. This can help create and maintain a productive relationship, which can in turn allow you to focus on your art.

Marci A. Rolnik
Legal Director, Lawyers for the Creative Arts

Chapter 1

Rights in What You Write

What you write down on paper or save on a thumb drive or hard drive is your valuable intellectual property, and is protected under federal copyright law. Whether it is a haiku or a novel, film script or blog post, what you write is, with few exceptions, protected by copyright. The requirements for protection are straightforward and simple:

- Your writing is "fixed" in a tangible "medium of expression."
- Your work is "original."

If your work meets these two criteria, it is copyrightable. There are several broad categories of works, however, which are not protected by copyright law, including:

- Words or short phrases
- Facts (other than compilations of facts, where the selection and arrangement of facts may be copyrightable)
- Ideas or concepts
- Methods of operation, processes, or systems

Unfortunately, your great idea for a novel or film—such as a plot, set of characters, or style twist—is not of itself protectable. However, the *expression* of this idea is copyrightable. The best way to protect this expression is to "fix it" in a tangible medium, that is, in some concrete form. "Tangible medium of expression" means that an expressive work has been placed on either an analog or digital medium—it has been written on a piece of paper, recorded on an audiotape or videotape, or stored on a computer disk or hard drive.

Only then will your expression of an idea be protected by copyright: your specific take on the plot, the characters, the story structure, and so forth. Telling the world what a great idea or concept you have will not make it yours;

spreading this idea around will only increase the chance of you feeling "ripped off" later when someone else comes up with a similar idea. The law will protect what you literally wrote down, but the scope of that protection will be limited to what you did in fact write down.

Chapter 2

A Copyright Owner's "Bundle of Rights"

As the author of a work, you are the owner of the copyright. A copyright is best described as a "bundle of rights" which only you can exercise or authorize someone else to exercise. These rights are set forth in the Copyright Act at 17 U.S.C. § 106.

Reproduce the work

The right to "reproduce" a work is the right to cause copies to be made, whether by printing a copy or making a digital copy. This is the primary right many authors aspire to "sell" to a publisher, whether it is a book publisher, magazine owner, website, newspaper, or other entity that publishes works.

Prepare derivative works

"Derivative works" are those based on the original. The Copyright Act, for example, lists certain types of potential derivative works, such as a translation, musical arrangement, dramatization, fictionalization, motion picture version, abridgement, or condensed version. For instance, most novelists would be delighted if a film producer wanted to acquire the right to produce a "derivative" work based on the novelist's book.

Publicly distribute copies of a work

The right of "public distribution" is most often included in the right to "publish." Once a work is published, however, anyone who validly owns a physical copy of that work can transfer that copy (and that copy only) to another person. For example, you can sell used books without the author's permission. Readers cannot, however, make a copy of a downloaded book and sell it without the copyright owner's permission.

Publicly perform a work

A novelist has the right to read his or her work in public. An extended reading of a novel or short story for an audience other than in a teaching situation most likely is a public performance of the copyrighted work and must be authorized by the copyright owner.

Publicly display a work

The display right does not often pertain to published writings. However, if a short work such as a poem is displayed on a billboard or other place in a public setting, this right could conceivably extend to a piece of writing.

Publicly perform sound recordings by a digital audio transmission

This right, of course, does not pertain to writings. However, it is a right that is important to authors, as it pertains to audio books which are produced with the copyright owner's permission, to the extent the audio book is transmitted by means of a digital audio transmission, such as through an on-line streaming service.

As a general rule, if a third party does any of the above things without the permission of the copyright owner, that party is liable for copyright infringement. (What constitutes copyright infringement is discussed later in this book at Chapter 16.) As the copyright owner, you have the right to say "yes" or "no" to any request you receive to exploit any of these rights. If you say "yes," you have the right to negotiate a fee or royalty for that use, to limit that use in terms of geography or time, and to limit the media in which it may be used. There are a limited number of instances in which a third party may quote from your work or otherwise use it in limited ways without your permission. These will be discussed later in relation to fair uses of copyrighted materials.

Chapter 3

Copyright Registration

Copyright protection exists from the moment you "fix" your "expression." Strictly speaking, you do not have to put a copyright notice on your work, but it is a good idea. It is also necessary to register your copyright prior to filing a lawsuit in a United States federal court to enforce your copyright. Several standard ways exist how a copyright notice looks:

- Copyright, Year of First Publication of the Work, Author's Name
  - ➤ Copyright 2013 John Doe
- ©, Year of First Publication of the Work, Author's Name
  - ➤ © 2013 John Doe
- Copr., Year of First Publication of the Work, Author's Name
  - ➤ Copr. 2013 John Doe

If you are sending out a manuscript and want, as a matter of best practices, to include a copyright notice, you might use a legend like this (since you don't have a publication date yet):

- Unpublished material protected by copyright, John Doe

Again, you own a copyright to your work without registering it with the Copyright Office. Registration not only provides the world notice that you own a copyright in your work, but it is also a prerequisite to filing a copyright infringement suit. The Copyright Office provides forms and instructions for the registration of copyright in published and unpublished works. Registration can be accomplished online, and doing it this way is cheaper than by printing a form and mailing it in. The form for a literary work is form TX (which is available at copyright.gov/forms). The copyright application asks you for the following information:

- The type of work
  - ➤ Magazine article, novel, film script, theatrical script, compilation, anthology, etc.
- The title of the work
- Whether the work has been published, and if so, the date
- The author's name
  - ➤ Note that your employer, by virtue of the "work for hire" doctrine, may be the "author" of the work.
- The name of the person claiming copyright (the "claimant") and how that person claims copyright, for example:
  - ➤ By written contract
  - ➤ By will
  - ➤ By assignment
  - ➤ By transfer of all rights by the author (you do not attach transfer documents or contracts to the application)
- Any limit on the claim of copyright
  - ➤ If any of the material in your work was previously published or is not covered by the current claim of copyright in the work, then that prior existing material and its date of prior publication must be disclosed.
- A deposit copy
  - ➤ If you are registering your work online, you may deposit an electronic copy of unpublished works or works that have been published only in a digital format. If you are registering something that has been published on paper, such as a book or magazine, you most likely will need to submit two copies of the best edition of the work in hard copy form. The online system gives you instructions for printing an appropriate mailing label so that your work can be deposited with the Library of Congress.

After you have submitted your application, the Copyright Office reviews it and makes sure the application is complete. If it is complete and claiming copyright to copyrightable subject matter, the Copyright Office will send you a certificate of registration. Unlike a trademark application, the Copyright Office makes no independent evaluation about whether you are entitled to the copyright or whether your work is wholly original. The certificate indicates only that you have made a claim to be the copyright owner, and notifies the world of your claim—which can be useful, for example, if you are hoping to exploit rights in derivative works.

Registration is also "prima facie" evidence that your claim to copyright is valid. This means there is a presumption in your favor as to ownership of the copyright in a work, but only if the registration is made before publication or within five years after the date of first publication. If you register prior to or within three months of publication and before your work was infringed, then statutory damages and attorneys' fees will be available to you in court as remedies if you successfully pursue an infringer of your work in court. (And statutory damages are not insignificant, as they can range from $750 to $30,000 per work infringed at the discretion of the court, and up to $150,000 per work infringed for "willful" infringement.) In the absence of statutory damages, you may be eligible to recover only actual (*i.e.*, provable) damages and profits attributable to the infringement.

For certain categories of works, including literary works being prepared for publication in a book, the Copyright Office offers "preregistration." This category does not replace actual registration once a work is published, but is meant to assist in the protection of works which have had a history of infringement prior to authorized commercial distribution. To be eligible for preregistration, a work must:

1. Be unpublished; and

2. Be *in the process* of being prepared for commercial distribution, either in physical or digital format.

Preregistration is available online only, costs considerably more than standard registration, and is not a guarantee of future registration. It is simply a process that allows the owners of works likely to be infringed to have access to federal court as early as possible to stop early infringements. Publishers and producers of hugely popular series (think *Harry Potter*) are most likely to benefit from this preregistration procedure.

Chapter 4

Fair Use of Another Person's Material

The music industry didn't invent "sampling." Authors of both nonfiction and fiction have often been inspired by works which have come before them. Authors often use quotes from other books, poems, diaries, letters, songs, folklore, and photographs and illustrations from third parties in a work which is otherwise wholly original with them. What and how much an author can use is also a guide to how much of your work another person can use of yours. This is called "fair use."

While what constitutes "fair use" of a work is not explicitly defined in the Copyright Act, it does list several examples of fair use, including: criticism (such as a review of a work), commentary, news reporting, using the work in a classroom, scholarship, and research. Note that the scope of what is fair use in teaching has been narrowed by guidelines found in the legislative history of the Copyright Act, which are detailed in the number of words a teacher can copy from a given kind of work, the number of instances of multiple copying per term, and the number of excerpts from any given work. The guidelines make clear that teachers should not replace texts with photocopying or online delivery of articles without permission from the article copyright owners.

The general considerations for determining what is fair use are four factors set forth in the Copyright Act, which a court applies to determine whether or not a use is fair:

1. The purpose and character of the use (*e.g.*, whether for commercial or educational purposes):

   ←INFRINGING   **↔**   **FAIR→**

   Commercial   Educational, Nonprofit

2. The nature of the copyrighted work:

   ←INFRINGING   **↔**   **FAIR→**

   Fictional   Factual

3. The amount and substantiality of the portion used in relation to the copyrighted work as a whole:

   ←INFRINGING   **↔**   **FAIR→**

   Higher percentage   Lower percentage

4. The effect of the use upon the potential market for or value of the copyrighted work:

   ←INFRINGING   **↔**   **FAIR→**

   Replaces need for original   Consumers still want original

No bright line rule exists on what constitutes fair use, and courts are free to and sometimes do use other factors in their analysis. A publisher—if you have one—most likely will not make this determination for you. Rather, publishers are conservative about using material from another person's work, and will most likely require you to get whatever permissions are necessary to quote from another person's work. If you have doubts about whether using another person's work in what you are writing is fair or not, you should get advice from your lawyer. You might also ask yourself how you would feel if another writer took that much of your work. Simply put, would you feel flattered or ripped off? That might be your best guide to fair use.

Fair Use In Action
The Wind Done Gone: **The Case of *Suntrust v. Houghton Mifflin***

In 2001, the estate of author Margaret Mitchell, famous for writing *Gone With The Wind*, sued publisher Houghton Mifflin and author Alice Randall for copyright and trademark infringement related to Randall's book, *The Wind Done Gone*. The book is a reinterpretation of *Gone With The Wind* told from the perspective of a recently freed slave. Mitchell's estate petitioned a United States district court in Georgia to prevent publication of the book and for $10 million in damages.

The district court stopped Houghton Mifflin from publishing the book, but the United States Court of of Appeals for the Eleventh Circuit reversed, holding that Randall and Houghton Mifflin were entitled to a fair use defense. The Eleventh Circuit noted that, although Randall used copyrighted elements from *Gone With The Wind*—characters, setting, scenes, plot, and dialogue—she had transformed those elements to critique and parody the work.

Houghton Mifflin subsequently published *The Wind Done Gone*, which went on to become a New York Times Bestseller. The parties settled the damages aspect of the lawsuit in 2002, with Houghton Mifflin agreeing to make an unspecified contribution to Morehouse College.

Common Fair Use Questions

What is the "public domain" and may I freely copy from it?

The public domain is a term that refers to works not covered by copyright. The work may have been explicitly given to the public domain by its author (although that is uncommon) or may have lapsed into the public domain for failure to comply with the requirements of copyright under prior laws, or because the term of copyright has expired. There are some general rules of thumb to determine if a work is in the public domain. For example, a work is surely in the public domain if its author has been dead for more than 70 years or if a corporate or anonymous work was first created 120 years ago, or if the author's date of death is not known but the work was created 120 years ago.

May I quote a song?

In a work of fiction, stanzas of a song might be used as part of the setting or to introduce a chapter. You will need to consider the length of the song and how much of it is used. Typically, third-party publishers will ask that you get permission by writing to the publisher of the song to get a synchronization license to the song. Since song lyrics are typically short, a whole stanza could be considered a "substantial" taking, which may not be considered a fair use.

May I quote a poem?

Like songs, poems are typically short. A whole stanza can be a substantial taking, and even in the context of literary criticism, quoting a whole stanza of, say, a four-stanza poem may be considered a "substantial" taking.

May I quote from a book?

Because books are typically longer than songs or poems, it is possible to quote a line and possibly even a paragraph or more from a book under the protection of the fair use doctrine. Of course, if a work (like the Bible or any book first published in the United States prior to 1923) is in the public domain, you may quote from it extensively, although you cannot pass it off as your "original" work.

May I quote from a blog?

Because blogs are short, little can be taken without the taking being "substantial." However, because blogs are timely, rarely have an economic value or market of their own, and may be considered freely distributed for the purpose of being quoted, there may be less risk in quoting from a blog—although repeated quoting from the same blogger may amount to a substantial taking.

May I quote a famous saying?

You can quote Ben Franklin's aphorisms and probably also famous lines from celebrities in the context of either a nonfiction or fictional work. There may be privacy concerns or concerns about placing a person in a false light if you quote something someone said to you in private or if you put words in someone's mouth, but those are separate issues discussed later in this book.

May I quote from someone's letters?

Even if the letter is addressed to you, you do not own the copyright in that letter. The writer of the letter is the author and thus the copyright owner. Because letters are typically short, at most you could quote very little under the protection of the fair use defense; you will also need to consider privacy issues discussed later in this book.

May I quote from a diary?

Diaries are original works and the copyright is owned by the diarist. If the diary has never been published, it is protected for the life of the author plus 70 years. If you do not know when the author died, then copyright most likely exists 120 years from the date of creation. In 2013, an unpublished diary would be in the public domain if the author died before 1943 or if it was written before 1893.

May I use a copy of a picture or illustration I found online?

Like writings, photographs and illustrations are fixed in a tangible medium of expression and are protected by copyright, even when they appear on a website. Permission is almost always required to use a photograph. Photographs and illustrations have the same terms of copyright as other works, so the copyright lasts for the life of the photographer/illustrator plus 70 years, but 120 years from creation if the death date of the photographer is not known or the work is anonymous or attributed to a company. Photographs which are published on websites are not free simply because you are able to download them.

May I parody a well-known work?

Parodying a well-known work necessarily requires that the parodist use enough of the underlying work for the parody to be recognized, and the use of the other's work to create the parody is a derivative work. The parody may be considered a fair use if the parody comments on the original work and is not simply using a familiar rhythm or authorial voice to comment on something else. In addition, the parodist cannot take more of the original than is necessary to conjure up the original. The question of how much can constitute a parody is subjective, and is a question that can be best addressed by an attorney experienced in copyright law and issues of fair use. But to better understand what a parody is, take what the Supreme Court wrote in *Campbell v. Acuff-Rose Music*, which involved a rap parody of the Roy Orbison song "Oh, Pretty Woman":

> For the purposes of copyright law, the nub of the definitions, and the heart of any parodist's claim to quote from existing material, is the use of some elements of a prior author's composition to create a new one that, at least in part, comments on that author's works. If, on the contrary, the commentary has no critical bearing on the substance or style of the original composition, which the alleged infringer merely uses to get attention or to avoid the drudgery in working up something fresh, the claim to fairness in borrowing from another's work diminishes accordiWngly (if it does not vanish), and other factors, like the extent of its commerciality, loom larger. Parody needs to mimic an original to make its point, and so has some claim to use the creation of its victim's (or collective victims') imagination, whereas satire can stand on its own two feet and so requires justification for the very act of borrowing.

Granted, the Court did not provide a bright-line definition. But this helps to offer clarity in an area which can seem to have more questions than answers.

Chapter 5

Writing with Others—Collaborations and Joint Works

When you and your friend have a great idea and decide to write a book or screenplay together, you might be considered joint owners of the copyright in the work. Inevitably, one author claims to have a greater ownership stake than the other, either because it was "their idea" or they perceive themselves as taking the laboring oar or doing most of the promotion. Then conflict arises, in which two primary issues usually emerge: (1) is the work in fact a joint work; and (2) in what proportion should the parties share in the profits?

For a work to be a joint work, the authors must have worked together *with the intent to make a joint work*. Mere contribution to the work is not sufficient to create joint ownership of the work. For instance, when you write an article and submit it to an editor at a magazine, the editor may make some corrections, suggestions, and even some additions. When you created the work, you did not intend to create a joint work with any particular editor. However, it is not the custom in the industry for an editor or dramaturge to have a claim to joint authorship of a work.

When people work closely on a project, they may intend to create a joint work even though, by the nature of the work of writing, someone has to write a first draft of a section (or the complete work) to foster the collaboration. Therefore, it is imperative that writers who intend to collaborate on a work write and sign a binding contract between them prior to commencing work. This agreement should address several key issues:

- The intention to create a joint work;
- Tasks assigned to each author;

- Division of expenses in producing the work (here, it is easiest if each writer bears his or her own expenses, but if expenses are being shared, these need to be approved in advanced and each party should keep their receipts);
- Division of profits generated from the work;
- Credit and attribution—essentially, whose name goes first? Note that ghost writers often use a phrase such as "With co-Author," "As told to," or just have their name listed inside the book, and not on the cover; and
- Which party controls exploitation (licensing and/or sale) of the rights in the work?

Absent an agreement to the contrary, if a court believes that the parties intended to create a joint work, it is likely to find that the parties share equally in the proceeds of the work and that either party is free to grant a non-exclusive license to exploit the work, such as the adaptation of a screenplay or authorization to publish the work in a different format.

Of course, this would be less than ideal—besides one party losing control of the work, the division of revenues could become a source of contention. What started as a collaboration with promise could sour into a destructive relationship. As such, it is important to start the process of working with another writer with a clear understanding of the working relationship that you intend to create.

Minimally, your agreement should contain language which expresses the intent to create and jointly own a work, such as:

> Each of the parties to this Agreement agrees that he/she intends the Work to be a joint work and that each of them shall own an undivided 50% interest in the copyright in the Work.

Who Spawned These Characters?
The Question in *Gaiman v. McFarlane*

Award-winning author Neil Gaiman (*American Gods*, *The Sandman*) sued writer/artist Todd McFarlane in 2002 seeking a declaration that he jointly owned copyrights with McFarlane in characters created for the comic book *Spawn*. Gaiman claimed that he co-created multiple characters with McFarlane for *Spawn* # 9, and thus also held their copyright. McFarlane, for his part, argued that Gaiman contributed only the ideas for the characters, and ideas are not copyrightable.

The court, however, held that, although individual authors may contribute only ideas that would not on their own be copyrightable—for example, stock characters—the contributing authors may still be co-owners in the final copyrighted work. The Seventh Circuit went on to hold that Gaiman co-owned the copyrights with McFarlane.

Chapter 6

Writing for Others—Your Rights as an Employee

While copyright law goes to great lengths to protect the work product of authors and artists of all kinds, it does recognize a category of work that belongs to the one for whom the work was created. If you are employed full time by an employer and part of your job is to write articles or scripts, generate reports, create analyses, develop website content, or produce other copyrightable work, your employer owns the copyright in the work you produce. This is called a "work for hire." A "work for hire" has two primary parts:

1. It was produced by an employee

2. In the course of his or her employment.

Simply put, this concept helps employers invest resources into producing content with the knowledge that they own this content. For example, could you imagine if every writer and photographer in a newspaper owned the copyright to each of their articles or photos? It would create an unreasonable and most likely unworkable system of ownership.

Issues can arise, however, when the employer-employee relationship is not clear-cut, such as when an employee who is not necessarily engaged as a full-time writer for a company but nonetheless produces a copyrightable work the company wishes to use. Copyright law refers to the law of agency to determine whether an employer-employee relationship exists between the employer and the author of a copyrightable work. Certain factors then become important in determining whether an author-employee has created a work for hire for his or her employer:

1. **Control by the employer over the work**. Here, this factor weights toward being a work for hire if the employer determines how the work is done, has the work done at its offices, and provides equipment or other means to create the work.

2. **Control by employer over the employee.** A work may be considered a work for hire if the employer controls the employee's schedule in creating work, has the right to have the employee perform other assignments, determines the method of payment, or has the right to hire the employee's assistants.

3. **Status and conduct of employer.** If the employer is in business to produce such works, provides the employee with benefits, or withholds tax from the employee's payment, the work is most likely a work for hire.

If you create something in the course of your employment and during working hours, the copyright in your work almost certainly belongs to your employer. If you work full or part time in a creative business, chances are your employer owns what you write, even if you write it at home. Advertising agencies, corporate communications specialists, think tanks, and similar businesses will usually have policies in place that specifically address what part of your creative output they own. Such a policy might spell out that they own the advertising slogan you come up with at home, but not the novel you write on your "own" time.

Chapter 7

Writing for Others—Rights of Independent Contractors and Freelancers

If you are not employed by a company but nonetheless are contracted to do work for this company which involves the creation of copyrightable work, it is likely that the company owns the copyright in what your produce, either as a work for hire or by an assignment.

However, freelancers are not employees by the traditional sense of the word but are rather independent contractors. Copyright law defines a second class of work for hire as work by an independent contractor that is specially ordered or commissioned for use in one of nine categories *and* that the parties agree *in writing* is work for hire. The nine categories of works are:

1. A contribution to a collective work (such as a magazine);

2. Contributing to a motion picture or other audiovisual work;

3. Providing a translation of a work;

4. A supplementary work, which is prepared as a complement to a work by another author, such as an introduction, conclusion, illustration, chart, answer key for a test, table, appendix, index, explanation, revision, or commentary;

5. A compilation;

6. An instructional text, which is a literary, pictorial, or graphic work prepared for a publication and intended to be used in instructional activities;

7. Producing a test;

8. Answer material for a test; and

9. An atlas.

If a contract is not in place which acknowledges that the freelancer agrees that her work is a work for hire, then it is not a work for hire. The freelancer would retain ownership of the work, and the party commissioning the work would have only those rights it specifically acquired. Because ownership disputes inhibit a company's use of the work it paid for, most companies will issue purchase orders which recite work for hire language (even if it does not apply) and, in the alternative, language which assigns the copyright to the company. In a ghost-writing contract, for instance, such a clause might look like this:

> FREELANCER hereby agrees that all materials prepared by her for the BOOK will be prepared by FREELANCER as work for hire for CELEBRITY/COMPANY as that term is defined in the Copyright Revision Act of 1976, 17 U.S.C. §101, and that CELEBRITY/COMPANY owns all right, title and interest, including the copyright, therein. To the extent the BOOK or any materials may be deemed not to be work for hire, FREELANCER hereby transfers and assigns all of its right, title and interest, including the copyright, in the BOOK and materials to CELEBRITY/COMPANY.

In some industries, it is common not to grant an assignment, but to acquire only certain rights, such as "first serialization." This means that the company may commission an article for, say, a magazine, but only expect to get the right to be the first to publish the article (both online and in print) and authorize reproductions of the article as it appeared in the magazine. The author would retain all other rights of copyright, such as the right to collect all of her articles in a book. In this case, the company commissioning the work has not acquired copyright ownership, either by virtue of the work for hire doctrine or by assignment, but has acquired only a license to exercise the specified right.

The Copyright Act includes a mechanism to protect authors from having to live with poor deals they may have entered into when they had little negotiating power. As authors get more famous or develop a following, they may feel, as many artists do, that their early work was undervalued. The Copyright Act

What Difference Does It Make?

Since a company ends up with all rights anyway, what difference does it make if the author's copyright is transferred because it is a work for hire or because there is a written assignment?

There are two major differences in a company's ownership of a copyright it owns by virtue of work for hire and by assignment. First, if a company owns a copyright by virtue of the work for hire doctrine, the term of the copyright is 95 years from the date of publication or 120 years from creation, whichever expires first. On the other hand, if the work is not a work for hire, the copyright term is the life of the author plus 70 years.

Second, the company is the initial owner of the copyright, and therefore its rights cannot be terminated. If an author grants an assignment of her copyright to a company, the author can terminate that grant about 35 to 40 years after the grant, pursuant to special procedures outlined in the Copyright Act.

allows authors who, after January 1, 1978, assigned their copyright or granted any license under their copyright, to terminate that grant or license at any time during a five-year period beginning at the end of 35 years from the date of execution of the grant or the date of publication under the grant, or 40 years from the date of execution of the grant, whichever occurs earlier. Notice must be served between two and 10 years prior to the effective date of termination. Upon termination, all grants covered by the author's grant end, but rights in a derivative work continue to be utilized pursuant to the terms of the grant.

If you wish to terminate a grant you made which is now eligible for termination, you should consult with an attorney to make sure you employ the process properly. Note that the right of termination cannot be waived, even if you signed a contract which purports to have you waive this right.

Chapter 8

Defamation, Libel, and Invading the Right
of Privacy or Publicity

Both fictional and nonfictional works may refer to real persons, or may use characters based on real characters. "Unauthorized" biographies and memoirs raise special issues about the use of a person identifiable by name or context. It is best to obtain written permission whenever practical from each person whose name, likeness, or actual identity you may use in your writing. But of course, that is not always practical, and, short of libel or invasion of someone's privacy or right of publicity, authors are given broad protection under the First Amendment. A newspaper or magazine, for example, does not need to get permission to use a person's name in an investigative story. However, there are several ways in which, under Illinois law, an author can lose that protection for statements made about an individual, whether in fiction or nonfiction. These include:

- Libel (also referred to as defamation);
- Invasion of the right of privacy; and
- Infringement of the right of publicity.

If you write unfavorably about a real person, or use a real person's identity in a fictional setting, consulting with an attorney would be a good idea prior to publishing the work to gauge if you may be liable for any of these claims.

Libel

In Illinois, a person who brings a libel claim must prove a number of elements to succeed in their case. First, they have to prove that the author of the writing *made a false statement* about them in his writing. Note that this significantly narrows the scope of writings subject to a libel claim, which can emerge from only a statement of fact, because a statement of opinion cannot be proven true or false. Also, even if you do not name the person bringing the libel suit in your story, if those who know the person will recognize the statement as being about him or her, then that person has a right to sue.

Next, the statement has to be disclosed to a third party. In the context of a piece of writing, this means that the work has been published. Note that as long as the statement has been disclosed to one other person, the statement has been sufficiently disseminated to form the basis of a libel claim. Therefore, if the statement is posted on a blog, or even simply e-mailed to someone, it has been disclosed to a third party.

You also have to have been at least negligent in making the statement. This is the standard for a statement if the person bringing the libel claim is a private figure. The Supreme Court has established a much higher standard that a public official (such as a politician), public figure (such as a famous athlete), or someone involved in a matter of public concern must show to bring a libel claim. They must show that the writer (or publisher) acted with actual malice. That is, they either knew that the statement was false, or acted with a reckless disregard for the truth. A gray area exists on who is a public figure, and who is a private figure.

Under Illinois law, if you have "reasonable grounds" to believe that what you have written about a private figure is true, you will not be guilty of defamation. But if you knew it to be false or "lacked reasonable grounds" for your belief, you may be guilty of defamation. Note that quoting another person's defamatory statement, even if attributed to the source, can still be considered defamation.

Finally, the person bringing the claim must show that the publication of the statement has caused damage. This "damage" is more than being merely insulted or offended. Usually, the damage is cause by a false statement of fact that exposes him to hatred, ridicule, or contempt; lowers him in the esteem of his peers; causes him to be shunned; or injures him in his business or trade.

Illinois does recognize certain categories of statements which are so egregious that they are automatically considered defamatory (called defamation *per se*). These statements are such that their "defamatory character is obvious and apparent on its face and injury to the plaintiff's reputation may be presumed." For instance, a person bringing a defamation claim does not need to prove they are harmed if you falsely accuse them of committing a criminal offense; having a "loathsome" disease; accuse them of not being able to perform or not having integrity in their job, profession, or business; or statements imputing adultery or fornication.

Because of the First Amendment, a central tenet of our society is a free exchange of thoughts and ideas. Accordingly, Illinois courts recognize several defenses to defamation actions. One is the fair reporting privilege, under which a writer is entitled to rely on official public documents, statements made by public officials, and what is said from the witness stand or in a city council meeting as part of his reporting. Note, however, that the writer has to make clear the source of the statement.

Another defense is substantial truth. Truth is an absolute defense against defamation. In addition, minor factual inaccuracies will not create grounds for liability if they do not materially alter the substance or impact of the statement.

In addition, opinion and commentary are not actionable as being defamatory. The First Amendment allows a writer to voice opinions, criticize others, and comment on matters of public interest. You can even use hyperbole if it is clear that you are using rhetorical ploys. You can call someone a jerk, stupid, inept, an idiot (use your imagination here), and as long as it cannot be proven true or false, you should be protected.

But there are statements which fall into a gray area which should be avoided, such pervert, thief, liar, alcoholic, or addict. Also, you usually cannot use the word "allegedly" as a disclaimer to such a false statement to prevent liability, or similar disclaimers such as "in my opinion" or "the mayor said."

Invasion of Privacy

There is not just one way for a writer to "invade" another person's privacy. In fact, Illinois law recognizes three ways that a writer can be subject to liability for this claim:

1. Intruding upon a person's seclusion;

2. Publicly disclosing private facts about a person; and

3. Casting someone in a false light.

Each of these is a distinct cause of action, with different elements that a plaintiff must prove in his claim. First, take intrusion upon a person's seclusion. Although this tort is more often a problem for filmmakers using hidden cameras, there may be instances where an author has so trespassed on another's seclusion so as to make the author's intrusion actionable. In Illinois, a person claiming intrusion upon seclusion must show:

1. An unauthorized intrusion or prying into another's seclusion;

2. A reasonable person would be offended by that intrusion;

3. The writer revealed a private matter; and

4. The ***intrusion itself*** caused the plaintiff anguish and suffering. Note that if there is a publication of something private learned during that intrusion, this may be actionable as a public disclosure of private facts, which is a separate cause of action for invasion of privacy.

Generally, you are free to take pictures of people in a public place or to quote overheard conversations in a public place. The issue is whether a person has an expectation of privacy in his home or on other private property.

The next cause of action to consider is the publication of "private" facts. Illinois law prohibits public disclosure of "true, but highly offensive or embarrassing, private facts." A person claiming that a writer disclosed his private facts must prove first that the writer used his name, personality, or likeness. Thus, if the writer does not use a name in an article or book, the disclosed facts must be sufficient, by themselves, to identify the person without outside knowledge.

Is This Publication Legal?

May I depict my crazy Aunt Nellie in my memoir?

In addition to the interpersonal implications of including your crazy aunt in you memoir, you need to consider whether you are making a factual statement which could be considered defamatory or cast her in a false light, or whether you are disclosing any highly offensive, private facts about her. If you are satisfied that what you have written is true—or is a matter of opinion—you can proceed without her consent. If what you have written is problematic, remember that merely changing her name or the color of her hair is not going to eliminate potential liability. You might want to fictionalize your story as well.

Are disclaimers effective?

A common disclaimer in the front of much modern fiction and many television shows reads something like this:

> This is a work of fiction. The names of people, characters, companies, and/or events mentioned herein are fictitious and are in no way intended to represent any real individual, company, or event unless otherwise noted.

For the most part, courts will honor such disclaimers when a work does not otherwise purport to be a retelling of real events. Dramatizations of actual events that purport to portray facts should, like biographies, be based on the reasonable belief of the writer to avoid claims of defamation.

I use real people to add verity to my fiction. Is that OK?

This is a common practice, but again, if the portrayal of the person could cast them in a false light which would be offensive or which defames them, you could be liable. In other words, do not use your thriller to accuse the sitting mayor of embezzlement.

So do not assume that simply changing a person's name removes liability for this cause of action. The facts must be disclosed to the public (*i.e.*, published), and they must in fact be private, and are not of legitimate public concern or historical significance. Typical "private" facts include those about a person's finances, health, or sexual activity. Finally, the disclosed facts must be highly offensive to a reasonable person.

The third cause of action for invasion of privacy is casting a person in a "false light." This involves publishing details—including true details—about a person in a context that conveys a "misleading impression of the person's character." Public as well as private persons can be cast in a false light.

An example from photojournalism can help make this tort easier to understand. Take a photograph of a man talking with a woman on the street. A caption might misleadingly suggest that he is soliciting a prostitute or that she is a prostitute, both of which could be false. Or a photo may show a bystander on the street that accompanies a story about some sort of civil disobedience, such as looting.

Again, while the bystander may not be involved in the looting, the photo may in fact create the impression that they are breaking the law. Thus, they have been cast in a false light, as long as they can show that (1) they have indeed been cast in a false light; (2) the publication would be highly offensive to a reasonable person; and (3) the author portrayed the victim in a false light with "actual malice" or "with knowledge of or reckless disregard" for the falsity of the statements. As such, it is not an easy cause of action to prove.

The Right of Publicity

Illinois, like many states, recognizes a "right of publicity," which is, essentially, the right to exploit a person's name, likeness, and identity for commercial purposes. The Illinois statute protects the "publicity rights" of persons both living and deceased, and protects a person's name, signature, photograph, image, likeness, or voice. The statute prohibits the use of a person's identity in connection with selling any product, merchandise, goods, or services; advertising any product, merchandise, goods, or services; and fundraising. However, a biography writer does not violate her subject's right of publicity by publishing an "unauthorized" biography.

Further, the statute does not prohibit use of a person's identity for non-commercial purposes such as news stories, public affairs, or sports broadcasts;

political campaigns; a single work of fine art; or a play, book, article, musical work, film, radio, television or other audio, visual, or audio-visual work. In other words, even though you sell your book or charge admission to your film, your work product is not necessarily "commercial" and does not violate the subject's right of publicity. This is where the right of publicity and the First Amendment co-exist. Note, however, that if an author otherwise misrepresents the work as being "official," "authorized," or "endorsed" by the subject, a violation of the publicity right could occur.

Chapter 9

Hiring and Firing a Literary Agent

While writers often submit their stories or poems directly to magazines and journals, book writers almost always need an agent. A possible exception is nonfiction, which, if targeted to a specialty market, may be submitted directly to a publisher. For most authors, getting a literary agent is the first step toward publication. Many helpful books and websites offer advice on whom to approach as an agent, and how to solicit their services. It is not unusual for an author to solicit more than 20 agents before finding one who will take her on.

When an agent represents you, they present your works to editors at publishing houses who they think are interested in your writing. Agents may charge you for out-of-pocket photocopying costs, retyping, long distance calls, and messenger fees, but only if you agree. According to the canons of the Association of Author's Representatives, they should not charge you for reading and evaluating your work, and they should not take a percentage from copy editors or book doctors to whom they may refer you. The author and the literary agent may agree on compensation to be paid to the agent, which frequently is a percentage, such as 15 percent.

The agent-author relationship is a personal one, and should be set forth in writing. That written contract, often in the form of a letter sent by an agent and signed by the author, should, at a minimum, cover several key elements.

Key Elements of an Author-Agent Contract

- Exactly which works the agent will represent and which rights the agent will represent, such as all rights, or only U.S. publications or foreign publication.

- The time during which the agent will represent the author, and the notice that either party must give in advance of termination. Contracts often have 30-day termination clauses.

- The method of computing the agent's compensation. If a publisher to which your agent has presented your book buys it relatively soon after you have terminated your agent, your agent may nonetheless be entitled to some compensation for having made the introduction and taking steps toward the publisher purchasing the work.

- Which expenses the author may be responsible for, and when the author will pay these expenses.

- Because the agent will receive advances and royalties from the publisher on your behalf, the "legalese" in the letter agreement will state that the agent has a fiduciary duty to you the author. As such, the agent should be required to keep your funds in a separate account, which is not co-mingled with the agent's own money. In addition, the agent should pay you within 10 days after the check from the publisher clears.

The agreement will typically include a very simple statement of appointment, such as:

> For the term of this Agreement, AUTHOR grants AGENT the exclusive right to represent AUTHOR in any and all negotiations for the sale of the Manuscript(s) and its subsidiary rights in all forms and media throughout the world.

It would also be typical for the agreement with the literary agent to include language like:

> AGENT shall have the right to receive commission compensation as set forth in this Agreement on any compensation AUTHOR receives arising out of the publication of the Manuscript(s) under a contract procured by the AGENT, whether or not that compensation is received after the termination of this Agreement, so long as the publication agreement was procured by the AGENT.

Some agents require a clause allowing the publisher to send two checks, one payable to the agent directly in the amount of the agreed commission. A paragraph like the following permits that "automatic deduction" to occur:

> AUTHOR agrees to include a provision in every Contract with Publisher(s) during the term of this Agreement, requiring the Publisher(s) to pay fifteen percent (15%) of all compensation under that Contract directly to the AGENT.

If you have to terminate your agent, you should consult the terms of the letter agreement. It may specify that you deliver the notice of termination with a return receipt or other special delivery mechanism. Ideally, you want a delivery method that can verify that the notice was delivered. Your letter should be polite, refer to the exact contract (by date) you are terminating, and specify the date of termination (which should concur with the requirements of the underlying contract). Unless otherwise specified in your agreement, there is no need to give a reason for the termination, and in the long run it may be preferable that you not burn any bridges by blasting the agent in your termination letter.

Chapter 10

The ABCs of a Publishing Contract

So, your agent has done her job and has landed you a deal to publish your novel. What should not be lost in this excitement of being published, however, is that now comes a critical part of the publishing process—the publishing contract! One of the most important documents an author can ever sign is a publishing contract. To help navigate what this document is and the process of negotiating and signing this contract, we will look at key terms in a book publishing contract and then in a standard magazine contract.

Grant of Primary Rights

The grant of rights clause typically grants the publisher the exclusive right to publish your work. But the rights may not be all-encompassing. For example, the rights may be for a specific language (for example, English or Spanish), in a particular format (in print or as an e-book), or in a specific territory (such as North America). Any rights an author does not specifically grant to a publisher belong to the author. You should attempt to keep the copyright in your work in your name, even if you grant all rights to the publisher. Major publishers, however, may insist on all rights, believing that they are in the best position, for instance, to negotiate foreign rights or movie rights.

Grant of Subsidiary/Ancillary Rights

Subsidiary or ancillary rights are related to the primary rights in a book. They include print-related rights such as translations; book club editions; selections, condensations, or abridgements in anthologies or textbooks; and first and second serial rights to publish selections of the book in magazines or newspapers either before or after publication of the hardcover version of your book. There are also subsidiary rights that are not related to printing your book, such as electronic rights (when these are not included in the primary grant), motion pictures and television, audio books, merchandising, and stage/ theatrical rights. Typically, an author and publisher split proceeds 50/50 of any exploitation of these subsidiary rights, which often involves licensing these rights to a third party, such as a film studio.

Delivery and Acceptance

Most agreements will require the author to deliver a manuscript "satisfactory to the publisher in form and content," and to do so by a specific date. The decision as to whether your manuscript is satisfactory is highly subjective, and the publisher has considerable discretion. This clause is of more concern to writers of nonfiction than fiction, since most novels are purchased after they are complete. Most nonfiction, on the other hand, is bought based on a proposal and sample chapter, which makes the satisfaction and delivery clause more important. At the very least, a publisher should be required to give the author of a rejected manuscript a written critique and a chance to revise the work.

Publication Date

Authors should make sure that their publication contracts obligate the publisher to actually publish and distribute their work by a certain date. If the publisher fails to meet that deadline, then the rights to the work (1) should automatically revert back to the author and (2) the author should get to keep any advance she has been paid.

Advance and Royalties

An "advance" is an upfront payment by the publisher to the author. It is a payment in anticipation of royalties that would otherwise be payable by the publisher to the author, and is usually payable in several installments: (1) on execution of the publishing contract; (2) delivery of the final manuscript; and (3) acceptance and publication. Ideally, the advance is nonrefundable, except in the case where you fail to deliver a manuscript.

Royalties are stated as a percentage of the retail list price of each copy of the book sold (in the case of large publishers), or, in the case of smaller publishers and for certain markets—including children's book and textbooks—as a percentage of the actual amount the publisher receives. Typically, a publisher sells books to the retail trade at a discount of 55 percent off of the retail sales price. If, for instance, your royalty is 10 percent of list, and the list price is $10, you would earn $1. If your royalty is 10 percent of the publisher's take, your royalty would be 10 percent of $4.50, or 45 cents.

Note that royalties may be scaled. For instance, you might earn 10% of the retail price of the book on the first 5,000 copies sold, 12.5% of the retail price on the next 5,000 copies sold, and 15% of the retail price on all copies sold thereafter.

Also note that "suggested retail list price" is a firm number, but "invoice price" is not. "Invoice price" is the list price minus freight charges. Also, if your contract offers a royalty based on "net proceeds," then you would specify exactly which expenses a publisher can subtract from the proceeds before calculating your royalties. These could include taxes, shipping charges, returns, and administration and marketing fees. Publishers will often include a contract provision that allows them to pay a lesser percentage on books for export, book club, mail order, or other special sales. The types of sales and the reduction of the royalty, however, are negotiable.

Accounting and Payments

A standard clause in a publishing agreement is one that is clearly important: how often you will be paid. This clause establishes how often your publisher must "account" to you regarding the proceeds from the sale of your book and any subsidiary rights income. Usually this accounting is twice a year. Note that in the first year or so, you will receive a statement but probably not a check, because your advance has not yet "earned out." You will get a check only after the royalties on sales exceed the amount of your advance. Sometimes, your publisher may owe you royalties but will also be entitled to withhold a "reserve" against possible future returns of your book. This reserve should be limited to a percentage of the royalties otherwise due, such as 20 percent of the past six months' royalties.

In addition, to ensure the accuracy of an accounting, your publishing contract should include an "audit clause," which gives you or your representative (such as your accountant, lawyer, or literary agent) the right to examine the publisher's books and records. If you conduct an audit and discover a significant discrepancy between the publisher's statements and your inspection of their records, the publisher is typically required to reimburse you for the costs of the audit in addition to paying the difference. What constitutes a "significant" discrepancy is negotiable. Further, any discrepancy should be paid within 10 days of when you give the publisher notice of the discrepancy.

Out of Print

Your publisher should only have the exclusive rights to your work while it is actively marketing and selling your book, *i.e.*, while your book is "in print." An "out-of-print" clause allows you to terminate the contract when copies are no longer available under a specific grant of rights, such as when the book is no longer for sale in the United States in an English language hardcover or paperback issued by the publisher. "Available for sale" usually means it is listed in the publisher's catalog. With the advent of print-on-demand and electronic versions, a book technically may never be out of print, and so it is common now for the out-of-print clause to be written instead in terms of the minimum amount of royalties which must be earned during each accounting period for the book to be considered in print. Once a book is deemed out of print, all rights in the book should revert to the author, even if the book has not earned out the advance.

Author's Representations and Warranties

An author or her agent who skips over the representations and warranties as mere legalese does themselves or his client a disservice. As the author, you should clearly understand the statements that you are being asked to make about your book, as these have significant consequences if you cannot make such a claim. Some common representations—which may look familiar in light of previous chapters in this book—are:

- You are the sole author of the book;
- You are the sole proprietor of the book;
- You are the sole owner of the copyright in the book;
- The work is your original work;
- The book has not been previously published;
- Rights to publish the book have not been previously granted;
- Any necessary licenses have been obtained, such as rights to photographs and illustrations or rights to quote substantially from another's work;
- The work is not libelous;
- The work does not invade the privacy rights of any person; or
- The work does not invade any other proprietary right (including publicity) of any person.

Author's Indemnities and Insurance

Representations and warranties have teeth because a contract will usually make it an author's duty to indemnify the publisher if a representation or warranty is false. If you promise to "indemnify and hold the publisher harmless" from any claims or lawsuits, typically you are required to hire the lawyer and defend the lawsuit. The author would control settlement of the lawsuit unless the publisher writes an indemnity clause that says the publisher can control the defense and/or veto any settlement. Lawsuits are expensive, and beyond the means of most authors. Therefore, the lawyer or agent negotiating your publishing agreement can attempt to limit the amount of money you might have to pay to the publisher in the event of litigation, such as not more than the sum of your advance and any royalties paid or 50 percent of the final judgment awarded a third-party plaintiff.

Other clauses can help protect you in the event of a lawsuit. You should make sure that you will not owe the publisher for any incidental damages or consequential damages, such as stock price dips due to a large judgment against a publisher or a famous author leaving the publisher because of the suit. Another clause should require the publisher to pay half the costs of defending a suit if you win the case. Further, a clause should exist that limits the amount of royalties the publisher can withhold if a lawsuit is filed.

An author could purchase insurance to protect himself against a third-party claim. However, it is usually much less expensive if the publisher will agree to name the author as an additional insured on the publisher's insurance, and charge this expense to the author. Because publishers typically cover large deductibles, some publishers will also limit the amount the author must contribute to a defense before the deductible is reached. For instance, a publisher may require an author to pay up to 20 percent of his advance for infringement and libel damages and attorneys' fees. If the suit is successfully defended, the publisher may want the author to pay half of the attorneys' fees and expenses. Ideally, these are covered by insurance.

Right to Sue for Infringement

Typically, if the publisher feels that the author's copyright is being infringed, it may request the right to sue the third party for infringement. Such a clause may require that the author consent to the lawsuit or even to pursue a potential suit. If a contract states that the costs of a lawsuit are to be charged to the author, then the author should have the right to agree in writing to the particular suit. If the author pays half the costs, any judgment or settlement should also be split 50-50. If the author does not pay the expenses of the lawsuit, it is common for a publisher to reimburse itself for expenses and lost sales, and then pay the author a portion of the recovery.

Publisher's Obligation to Promote

Typically, publishers have discretion over how to promote the book. They may also have complete control over designs used in promotions, such as the cover, jacket copy, website text, and press releases. First-time authors should be able to get some standard commitments from a publisher regarding promotion, including inclusion in the publisher's catalog, a certain number of complimentary review and promotional copies, and a commitment from the publisher that it will promote and not allow the book to go out of print for two years. There are certain promotional considerations that new authors will probably not be able to get from a publisher, but it is worth asking for them. These include the publisher booking and paying for a promotional tour, hiring and paying for a publicist, and committing to and spending an advertising and marketing budget.

Right to Revisions

The right of the author to have the first opportunity to do revisions applies to nonfiction works and textbooks. Usually, the publisher has the right to request a revision, and if the author cannot or does not deliver, then the publisher can engage another writer, and pay a portion of the royalty to the other author for the revisions. At some point, a book may be so revised that it is no longer a revision but an entirely new effort. If the new version is not the work of the original author, the original author may want to negotiate to have her name taken off the work.

Another important point regarding revisions is whether, for royalty purposes, the publisher counts the new revision as "sales" of the first version, or whether the clock is reset at zero. This matters if the royalty is a sliding scale, with higher royalties at higher thresholds of sales.

Option for Next Book

A writer would be delighted if a publisher seeks the option to buy her next work. This usually means that the author must offer her second book to the publisher, which would then make an offer, including an advance and royalties. The author can then accept or reject this offer at her discretion. If the option is written as a "right of first refusal," then the author could not sell her second book to another publisher at a price less than what the first publisher originally offered, without going back to the first publisher to match or decline to match this offer.

Hidden Rights Fees

For certain kinds of works, the licensing of elements to include in a book such as artwork, photos, and maps can be expensive, and you should try to get these expenses covered by the publisher in the contract. In addition, if the publisher demands an index, you should note that a professional index is expensive (even with modern technology), and you should try to get the publisher to pay for it, or at least contribute to it and charge the expense against your advance.

Assignment of Rights/Obligations

If your book is successful, you may reasonably expect to receive a royalty stream. You are entitled under most publishing contracts to assign the royalty stream to whomever you want, provided you give the publisher notice. However, a publisher typically cannot assign its publishing contract and the services it owes you without your permission, although some contracts will say that they can freely assign the contract to an "equally reputable publisher" or upon merger or acquisition. You should try to retain the right to get your work back if the publisher goes bankrupt.

As an author, your publishing agreement is the most important document you will sign. We have not included a model publishing contract here because each publisher's standard contract will be different depending on the type of work, the potential market for subsidiary rights, the fame of the author, and a variety of other factors. You will want your literary agent and attorney to comment on the specific legal language and to explain any terms that affect your rights and potential income from the publishing deal.

Chapter 11

Self-Publishing Basics

Self-publishing can be a satisfying and affordable way for an author to get his work out to the public.

The term "self-publishing" is generally used today to describe a form of publication in which the author pays the costs. In earlier years, this was often called "vanity" or "subsidy" publishing; today, there are a wide variety of self-publishing options available. Some self-publishing is the equivalent of outsourcing all or most of your production requirements: a cover, interior design, editing, ISBN, distribution through a national book distributor which sells to retail outlets, listing on electronic commerce sites such as Amazon.com and barnesandnoble.com, printing, etc.

These services are offered on a fee basis. Some will also take a percentage of their sales and pay the author what they term a "royalty." Some offer additional marketing services and options such as hardcover and e-book production on an a la carte basis. Some may not charge a fee, but will require an up-front minimum purchase commitment and will take a percentage of future sales. Other self-publishing options do not take a percentage, but simply charge for services and for the print run.

Other self-publishing models are strictly do-it-yourself, and most often print-on-demand. They print exactly what you give them, and they charge you only for the number of copies you order. Copies are produced on an "as-ordered" basis. They may offer distribution on their own sites or the e-commerce sites, in which case they will take a percentage of third-party orders for their print and fulfillment services. Some of the better known self-publishing companies are: Author Solutions, Booktango, CreateSpace, Dog Ear Publishing,

Hillcrest Media Group, Infinity Publishing, iUniverse, Lightning Source, Lulu, Outskirts Press, PublishAmerica, Tate Publishing, Trafford Publishing, Wheatmark, Xlibris, and Xulon Press.

Without some professional advice, self-publishing can be disappointing, both in terms of the quality of the product and your ability to market it effectively. Most self-publishing services available online use a click-through form agreement, and it is important than you understand it. Many of the terms will be like those discussed above regarding traditional publishing contracts, but you will want to pay special attention to licensed rights, printing costs, royalties, return of production files, and other issues such as delivery dates, design responsibilities, and turn-around times. Resources such as "The Fine Print of Self-Publishing" by Mark Levine are available to help compare the various options and programs available.

Licensed Rights

In the self-publishing context, most companies take only a non-exclusive right to publish the work. They are essentially providing you a printing (and perhaps a listing) service. You should never grant film or television rights to someone you do not know to be qualified in those areas.

Printing Costs

You should shop around. Be aware of what the going per-page print-on-demand rate is for a standard paperback. Printing costs are important because of how they are used in royalty calculations and whether the publishing company "marks up" (adds a percentage) to the printing cost they charge to you.

Royalties

Try to avoid "net" royalty calculations unless you understand the deductions from revenues prior to the royalty calculation. Be wary if printing costs are marked up before they are backed out of the net royalty calculation. In other words, do the math:

Example 1: 50% Royalty on net—publisher backs out actual print cost
$ 15.00 (retail price)
   -3.90 (actual print cost)
$ 11.10 (profit)
   x .50 (split fifty-fifty)
$ 5.50 author royalty

Example 2: 50% Royalty on net—publisher backs out actual print cost, print cost marked up
$ 15.00 (retail price)
   -7.80 (actual print cost =100% mark-up)
$ 7.20 (profit)
   x .50 (split fifty-fifty)
$ 3.60 author royalty

Example 3: 35% royalty on retail
$ 15.00 (retail price)
   x.35 (35% royalty)
$ 5.25 author royalty

Example 4: 25% royalty on retail
$ 15.00 (retail price)
   x.25 (25% royalty)
$ 3.75 author royalty

Return of Production Files

Most self-publishing contracts do not include a clause for the return of the original production files, which today typically are made in Adobe InDesign. While your publishing contract may give you a .pdf file, be aware that this is usually low resolution and not print ready. This means that if you switch to a new self-publisher, you will have to start over, since you will not have access to the production files.

Common Areas of Dispute

Several common problems exist in the self-publishing arena. For example, you may think that the publisher has failed to edit the text adequately. However, editing the text and putting it in the proper format is the author's responsibility. Simply put, you cannot blame your self-publisher for errors that you should have found at the electronic or physical proof stage. Similarly, image reproduction can sometimes be poor. Again, it is the author's responsibility to know the resolution required by the printer for the proper printing of digital images. Similarly, it is the author's responsibility to meet any deadlines the publisher makes to meet a targeted publication date.

In general, it is also the author's responsibility to market her book. Self-publishing fees do not cover marketing. Examine marketing packages that may be available to purchase for an additional fee from a self-publisher, and make sure you understand how much, if any, special attention your book will receive through this package. The extent of the marketing may simply be that it will be listed with all the self-published books the company produced that month. Realize that failure to sell copies does not mean that the marketing program you purchased did not happen; it could just mean that the program did not produce the results you wanted. Note that even traditional publishers rely heavily on authors to market their works. As such, it is important to develop your own marketing platform and use social media, local book stores, and your friends and family to help spread the word.

Finally, problems can emerge with getting paid. When it comes to royalties with a self-publishing company, you must understand how to read a sales report to determine if there has been a proper accounting. For example, know that a sale or two on Amazon.com can change your day's rankings by 100,000 places. Of course, this does not necessarily mean that you will see a huge rise in royalties or that your publisher is holding back on you.

Chapter 12

Publishing Articles in Magazines and on the Internet

You own the copyright in what you write, so you have the right to control the method of publication. You can try to publish a book, make copies at a photocopy machine, or post a blog on the Internet. You can try to charge to have access to your words, or you can distribute your work freely. There are thousands of magazines looking for content from freelance writers, which can often be a good source of revenue and recognition for a writer. It is important to keep a few key issues in mind when working with a magazine editor to have your stories published.

First, when a magazine purchases your story—if you are a freelancer and your work is not considered a "work for hire" as discussed in Chapter 7—the magazine acquires only the rights specified in the contract you have with the magazine. Common rights that a magazine will acquire are "first serialization" rights. These give the magazine the right to publish the article for the first time. They may be limited by language or by territory, such as "first North American serial rights" or "first English-language serial rights." After that publication, you may sell "second serial rights" or "reprint" rights, or you may repurpose the content, such as selling an anthology of similar articles or a book.

"Electronic rights" should be specifically addressed in a magazine contract. When periodicals first sought to make their content available online as well as in print, huge issues arose over whether the periodicals had the necessary rights from freelancers to make electronic copies of their works. Many had no paperwork with frequent freelancers, or, because the Internet did not yet exist or was in its infancy at the time of the contracts, the publications had acquired only one-time or first serial print rights. Today, the National Writers Union recommends a contract for freelance work in which the publisher acquires "one-time North American hard-copy print publication rights only." All other rights, including the electronic reproduction, transmission, display, performance or distribution of the article, CD-ROM, database, archive, proprietary services, and other electronic rights should be, according to the Writer's Union, fully reserved by the author and negotiated separately. In reality, however, many publications insist on acquiring these ancillary rights when they purchase an article, and will not work with a freelancer who refuses to provide them these rights. It comes down to a business decision for a writer: how much do they want to write for a certain publication and get paid, versus the control they want to have to further exploit their works.

The Union recommends a payment equal to the original payment for the additional use of the author's work in the publisher's electronic outlet for the course of that webpage's publishing cycle. For database use, the Union suggests a rate of 50 percent of the original fee per year. These could be uses separate from an archived copy of the magazine stored electronically.

Key Freelance Contract Terms

There are several important terms that should be included when you sell your freelance story to a magazine. Always make take sure that the contract includes language about:

- The specific rights the magazine is acquiring
- The length of the article
- The due date
- Your fee
- What expenses, if any, the magazine will cover
- A "kill fee"—the payment from the magazine if, after delivery, the editor chooses not to publish the article. (You will then be free to sell the piece elsewhere.)

From a copyright point of view, leafleting and blogging are the same activity. You keep your copyright, but you make it difficult to prevent infringements. In fact, by leafleting or blogging, you are arguably encouraging others to pass on your copy. Passing on a physical copy of the leaflet, much like giving away a used book, is not an infringement of copyright, and sharing a link to a site where someone has posted a blog you like is likewise not a copyright infringement, but technically, cutting and pasting an article from another page onto yours is an infringement, because it is making a copy.

When publishing content on a social media website like Facebook or Twitter, it is particularly important to carefully read the terms and conditions. You should pay particular attention to whether the site or service allows you to retain the copyright to your content and what sort of license you are granting to your intellectual property by posting on the website. Words like irrevocable, perpetual, worldwide, transferable, and sublicense rights are red flags that you may be losing control over the content you publish.

Also look for limitations to the license. For example, will the license end when you remove the content or delete your account, and how long will the content be stored after you delete it. Individual applications associated with social networking sites may have their own terms and conditions as well, and you should pay close attention to these. Finally, sites and services amend and change their terms and conditions from time to time. By continuing to use the site or service, you agree to any changes or amendments.

When writing for a website, the same considerations apply as when you are writing for any other business or publication. If you are producing content as an employee or under a work-for-hire agreement, the website's owner will own all the rights to the content you create. On the other hand, in the absence of an employment relationship or work-for-hire agreement, you will retain the copyright to your content but you should pay careful attention to what rights you are licensing to the website.

Additionally, technology now makes it easy to combine materials in various mediums into a single, multimedia product. If you decide to publish your book on the web using multimedia content and want to use third-party materials like music or photos, the first two principles you need to remember are: (1) works, even on the Internet, do not need to be registered with the U.S. Copyright Office to be considered copyrighted material; and (2) just because a work does not contain a copyright notice does not mean it is not copyrighted. This means that much of the third-party material you may want to use in your product is protected by copyright. If you did not specifically create the material that you use, you will need to make sure that the material is in the public domain or that you have contacted the copyright owner and acquired the rights through a valid agreement. Some uses may be subject to a fair use defense, as discussed in Chapter 4, but when in doubt it is best to make sure you obtain the necessary permissions.

On the flipside, if someone else uses your copyrighted materials online without your permission, it is possible that they are infringing on your copyright, and you might consider taking action to protect your rights. Before taking action, however, you will want to consider whether the use could be considered a fair use. Selective quoting and paraphrasing are probably fair uses of your copyrighted material, but wholesale copying and republication are not. Additionally, you should determine whether you have granted any license that would allow the reproduction of your work.

If you determine that someone is infringing on your copyright, the easiest and most straightforward approach is to email the website operator directly, stating that the site is infringing on your copyright and asking the operator to take down the infringing content. Contact information for website operators can often be found directly on the website itself. If that does not work, you can contact the website's service provider. The site whoishostingthis.com can help you determine the service provider. Once you determine the service provider, you will need to send your notice to that provider's registered copyright agent. The U.S. Copyright office maintains an up-to-date listing of registered copyright agents on its website. You will also need to include the following items in your notice:

- An identification of your copyrighted work that is being infringed;
- An identification of the material that you claim is infringing;
- Your contact information (address, telephone number, or e-mail address);
- A statement that you have a good faith belief the material is not authorized;
- A statement that the information you provided is correct and you are the copyright holder; and
- A physical or electronic signature.

At this point, the service provider will probably take down the infringing material. The person whose work has been taken down may then send a counter-notice to the service provider. If this happens, you will have 10 business days to file a lawsuit and notify the service provider that you have done so.

Chapter 13

Rights in Characters and Derivative Works

Long after we have forgotten a plot, we often remember a character from a well-written story. And with many popular characters, we can look forward to their future adventures. The author who creates such a memorable character has a valuable piece of intellectual property. While anyone can write a detective novel, only Sara Paretsky (or someone authorized by her) can write a V.I. Warshawski novel. Similarly, while the plot of a novel might at its core be simple, a filmmaker cannot produce a movie based on that plot without the author's permission.

The right to authorize the creation of derivative works is potentially a very lucrative right of owning a copyright. If you write a novel or short story, for instance, a film, television show, play, or cartoon strip could be a derivative work. Other ancillary products could also fall under the derivative works umbrella, such as calendars, toys, T-shirts, and posters.

If a major film is made from an author's novel or story, the movie producers are most likely to administer the merchandising and tie-in rights. The author will want to share in all the profits the movie generates from all sources, including DVDs, view-on-demand, product placements, and merchandising, not just the box office. The author should also receive "back-end profit participation," which is a percentage of the overall profits. The percentage is likely to be small, but could be significant. The critical issue is how profits or net profits are determined. This has often become the issue which gives rise to lawsuits.

In addition, a movie can generate a graphically recognizable character built on the author's written description of the character, through the general appearance of the actor, costumes, accents, mannerisms, or other physical features or characteristics depicted in the film. An author needs sophisticated legal advice to delineate her future rights to the character both as depicted in the movie (which might be a shared right) and in forms and appearances other than as depicted in the movie.

If an author is lucky enough to be approached by a film producer interested in making a movie based on her book, she will be asked to sign a "literary option agreement." This is not an agreement to actually make the movie; it just gives the producer a certain period of time (such as 12 to 24 months) in which to prepare an outline of the movie—referred to as a "treatment"—they want to make and to secure financing. During the option period, the producers can determine if the project could be profitable, and the author is not free to shop her book to other filmmakers. The option may be limited to English language, or for films to be distributed initially in the United States, or it may be for only an animated version. Usually, the producer who pays for an option for the film rights will protect itself against competing theatrical or foreign versions at the same time. When the literary option period expires, if the option has not been exercised in accordance with the terms of the agreement, then all the rights revert back to the author, who is free to sell the film rights to another producer.

A literary option agreement is often drafted in two parts: (1) the literary option, and (2) the literary rights agreement. Common terms in the option include the rights the producer acquires, how long the option lasts, the fee for the option (which is usually much smaller than the author might anticipate), the option price (the price the producer will eventually pay the author for the rights to make a film, when and if he or she exercises the option), the mechanism for exercising the option, and the possibility of extending the option for a second option period for an additional payment. Typically, the option looks like this, and references an attached literary purchase agreement:

> In consideration of the payment to Owner of the sum of $___, receipt of which is hereby acknowledged, Owner hereby grants to Purchaser the exclusive and irrevocable option to purchase from Owner the rights in the Property as described in the Literary

Purchase Agreement attached as Exhibit A for the total purchase price specified and payable as provided in Exhibit A. If Purchaser shall fail to exercise this option, then the sums paid to Owner hereunder with respect to the option shall be an remain the sole property of Owner.

The literary rights agreement referred to above is a more robust contract. Overall, it grants the producer the right to make the movie or other project based on the book. It specifies the price to use the author's work in the film, which may be a percentage of the film's final budget. A fee may state a minimum amount to be paid to the author—sometimes referred to as the "floor"—or the maximum fee (also called the "ceiling"). For example, an author may request that the purchase price be equal to a percentage—usually between 1.5 percent and 3 percent—of the final budget, with a floor. In addition, a producer may ask that the option price be credited against the purchase price, but such a clause is not to the author's advantage.

An author will also want to have a clause in which she receives a portion of the profits generated by the production. Customarily, a producer will grant a net—as opposed to gross—profit participation. This typically falls around 5 percent of net proceeds. Note that the definitions of gross and net profits in the film industry are far from straightforward and can be tricky, so be wary of attempting to negotiate a film deal on your own. In addition, the owner can negotiate to receive box office bonuses payable if the movie generates a particular level of box office gross receipts. These clauses are particularly tricky and the author would be wise to rely on the advice of an attorney with respect to the contract language to make sure it reflects the author's understanding of how his or her profits will be calculated.

There are several other common clauses in a literary rights agreement. It will usually specify the credit the author will receive that accompanies the film, such as "based on the [Book Title] by Author." It will also usually specify the author's consultation rights in producing the film. Note, however, that most authors will not receive consultation or approval rights over creative aspects of the film or television project, such as the cast, director, or final screenplay. Usually, the producer will assume creative control.

Finally, the agreement should specify the rights an author retains. This is important, as an author may grant film rights and retain theatrical rights, but still be required to covenant that she will not grant the stage rights for a number of years after the film's release, which is called a "hold-back."

Chapter 14

Moral Rights

The concept of "moral rights"—an author's right to protect the integrity of her work—is common in Europe, and is written into many countries' copyright laws. In general, these rights protect the value that an author places in her work. For example, they provide the author the right to receive or decline credit for her work, or the right to prevent her work from being altered without her permission. Other areas of control exist with these rights. For example, a visual artist may be able to control who owns her work, and to determine if and where a work may be displayed. These rights may also extend to how an author gets paid, such as the right to receive royalties on the resale of their work.

In the United States, moral rights typically refer to the ability of an author to claim that she created this work; to prevent the use of her name in conjunction with a work she did not create; to prevent the use of her name with a work that could prejudice her honor or reputation; or to prevent the intentional destruction, modification, or alteration of her work. Under U.S. law, these rights are generally only enforceable through contract or statute.

- **Requiring use of an author's name**: The prevailing view in the United States is that an author who sells or licenses her work does not have any inherent right to be credited as the author of the work absent contractual provisions. As such, an author who wants to retain this right should be certain to make sure that any contract licensing or selling her work contains a provision expressly requiring that the author's name accompany any reproduction of her work.

- **Preventing untruthful use an author's name**: In the United States, both court-made case law and federal trademark law protect an author from being attributed as the author of a work she did not in fact create. Even if an author assigns the right to make reasonable changes to her work, she may have a cause of action if those changes substantially depart from her original work, while still holding her out to be the author.

- **Preventing truthful use of an author's name**: In the absence of contractual provisions to the contrary, an author may not object to truthful statements that she is the author of a work that she has sold or licensed, unless the work has been substantially altered. An author may, however, have an action for invasion of privacy or defamation when truthful attribution of her name appears in conjunction with publication of an unpublished work that the author believed unworthy of publication.

- **Preventing distortion of an author's work**: In the United States an author may seek contractual remedies and possibly remedies for unfair competition under federal trademark law where a licensee distorts an author's work without authorization.

Illinois does not specifically recognize by statute an author's moral rights. However, if someone copies your work and signs their name to it, you are likely to have a cause of action under Illinois law for fraud, misrepresentation, or false advertising. If someone publishes your work without your permission, you have the right to sue for copyright infringement. If they fail to give you a byline, you may or may not have a cause of action under a common law theory such as unfair competition (passing off your work as theirs), depending on the circumstances. Some visual artists are able to claim broad rights in their unique style, but it is difficult for most authors to be able to claim a style so distinctive and instantly identifiable that imitation of their style would be actionable.

Buying an Argument for Moral Rights
Gilliam v. American Broadcasting Co.

In 1975, the British comedy troupe Monty Python sued ABC to prevent the company from broadcasting an edited version of the show "Monty Python's Flying Circus," which had originally been written and recorded for the BBC. Specifically, Monty Python objected to ABC's omission of approximately 27 percent of the original recordings in order to make room for commercials. Monty Python argued that ABC's heavy editing violated contractual provisions limiting the right to edit Monty Python material and also "constituted an actionable mutilation" of the group's work.

The United States Court of Appeals for the Second Circuit agreed. While the court noted that American copyright law does not protect moral rights per se, the court pointed out that contractual provisions and statutory remedies allowed Monty Python to enforce these moral rights in practice.

First, the court looked at the terms of Monty Python's original contract with BBC and found that because the contract did not allow BBC to alter the shows once recorded, BBC could not convey that right to ABC. Importantly, the court noted that the rationale for finding copyright infringement when a licensee publishes a truncated version of a work without authorization is to allow the copyright holder to control the method by which his work is presented to the public, and thereby preserve the quality, reputation, and economic value of the work.

Second, the court held that the unfair competition provisions in trademark law allowed Monty Python to sue for unauthorized "mutilation." This statute protects copyright holders from misrepresentations of their works that injure business or personal reputation. After watching and comparing the original and edited versions of the Flying Circus, the court noted that ABC's truncated versions often omitted from the skits elements essential to the Monty Python's "rare brand of humor," impaired the integrity of the work, and presented a "mere caricature of [the group's] talents." Based on this distortion, the court concluded that Monty Python had a valid cause of action for unfair competition under trademark law.

Chapter 15

Trademarks to Names, Titles, and Characters

While copyright does not protect book titles or author and character names, the law does protect titles and names as trademarks. A trademark is a word or symbol used in connection with goods or services to distinguish them from those of others. It has been said that a trademark answers the question, "Who are you?" rather than "What are you?" The title of a book can be thought of as the "what"—"I am the book entitled XYZ." The title of a series, however, can be thought of as the "who"—"I am a book in the series recognized as 'For Dummies.'" "For Dummies" can function as a trademark, while the name of a particular title cannot.

Sometimes, an author's name can function as a trademark. For example, Chicago chef Rick Bayless has registered his name as a U.S. trademark for cookbooks, and J.K. Rowling owns several trademarks to her name as they relate to books and other goods and services related to the *Harry Potter* series. A character's name may also be registered as a trademark, such as Nancy Drew.

Celebrities often offer their services under personal services corporations, which own their name or persona, and license out their names and their services. Those companies may formalize their ownership of the author's name through registration. Whether there are advantages to you in registering your name—and whether you have the rights to do so—are subjects for discussion with an attorney.

The United States has a dual system of trademark protection, both federal and common law, but both are dependent on actual use. A trademark owner develops rights in a trademark just by being the first to use it on a certain class of goods or services. Common law ownership of a trademark, sometimes evidenced by a state registration, allows the owner to prevent others from using a similar mark on similar goods or services, if the result would be confusion in the marketplace as to the source of the goods or services.

Federal registration confers additional valuable rights on the owner. Chief among these is the right to use the symbol ®. (If you see the symbol ™, that means that the owner claims it as a trademark; it doesn't indicate ownership of a federal registration.) In addition, federal registration provides constructive notice of a claim of ownership of the mark—after registration, a junior user cannot adopt the same mark in good faith because he or she is charged with notice of the registered mark. The registration is evidence of ownership of the mark and gives the owner access to federal court in the event of infringement.

The registration process is relatively easy and inexpensive, and can be accomplished online at uspto.gov. While an attorney is not required, a knowledgeable attorney can facilitate the process, which often takes as much as a year or more from application to registration.

Trademark infringement occurs when an identical or similar mark is used on an identical or related product in a manner that creates a likelihood of confusion among customers as to the source of the product. The "likelihood of confusion" has been interpreted to mean something akin to the "probability" that confusion will occur. Something more than a mere possibility of confusion must exist, although actual confusion is not required.

Your attorney should be able to make an informed judgment on the "likelihood of confusion" based on her experience in the field. If an infringement is occurring, your attorney can file suit in federal court to stop the infringement and possibly to recover damages for lost sales and profits.

Chapter 16

Protecting Your Work from Infringement

Beyond the value you place on your work, your writing can have real monetary value. This book has discussed many of the ways you can exploit your work. But what if someone else is using your work without your permission? Then you may have a claim of copyright infringement.

What is copyright infringement?

If a third party uses your writing in a way that is included in the "bundle of rights" you own as set forth in the Copyright Act, and does so without your permission, they may have infringed your copyright. For instance, if you own the copyright in a novel, any of the following would most likely—subject to several "fair use" exceptions—be an infringement if done without your permission:

- Photocopying the entire book or a chapter;
- Making a movie based on the book;
- Including a chapter in an anthology;
- Reading a chapter out loud at a public gathering; or
- Producing a stage play based on the book.

As the copyright owner, you may file suit to prevent the infringement from continuing and recover damages. As a plaintiff in that lawsuit, you must prove three things:

1. **You own the copyright**. You must register your copyright with the Copyright Office prior to filing suit, and the suit must be filed in a federal district court, as copyright is an issue of federal law, not state law.

2. **The defendant copied your work**. This can be established through either direct evidence, or evidence that shows that the defendant had actual or probable access to your work, and the defendant's work is substantially or strikingly similar to yours.

3. Copyrightable material was copied. This relates to the discussion in
Chapter 1 of this book. Remember that ideas, facts, generic plot lines,
historical scenes, or standard gags or bits cannot be copyrighted. The
phrase "scenes a faire" is sometimes used in this context. These are
words or images that are common to any story set in a certain time
or place, such as cotton fields in a story about slavery. Only original
expression can be registered as a copyright.

Third parties can sometimes use your work without your permission if the
way they exploit you work is considered a "fair use." Fair use is a defense to
your infringement claim. Again, and as discussed in more detail in Chapter 4, a
court will consider the following factors in determining whether the defendant
has made fair use of your work:

1. The purpose and character of the use (*e.g.*, whether for com-
    mercial or educational purposes);

2. The nature of the copyrighted work (whether it is a work of fic-
    tion or non-fiction);

3. The amount and substantiality of the portion used in relation to
    the copyrighted work as a whole; and

4. The effect of the use on the actual or potential market for or value
    of the copyrighted work.

A defendant may argue that your work is not covered by copyright, or that
he has only copied non-copyrightable matter. Or he may argue that his work
was an independent creation, and deny that he copied your work. If your work
is relatively unknown or not widely distributed, you may need to prove how
the defendant had access to your work. The less likely the access, the more
substantially similar the works must be in order for a court to conclude that
the defendant copied your work. In other words, what are the chances that two
writers would write a substantial number of paragraphs in a novel exactly the
same way, using the same words in the same order?

Damages for infringement

Two kinds of monetary recoveries are available if you succeed in your infringement suit. First, you are entitled to recover "actual damages" attributable to the infringement. These are calculated according to your lost profits, for example, the royalties you would have earned on a sale of that copy yourself, or what the normal payment to you would have been for the right to write and produce a film script.

Because actual damages may be difficult to prove, especially for self-published or short-run authors, "statutory damages" are available. These are damages awarded by the court, in its discretion, in the amount of $750 to $30,000 per work infringed. If a court believes that the infringement was deliberate or willful, it may award higher damages, up to $150,000 per work infringed. Statutory damages are available only from the date of registration, which is another reason why authors should register their copyrights as soon as possible after publication rather than waiting for the need to register when they want to sue.

Injunctions against future infringements

If someone infringes your work, you may also be entitled to an injunction, which is an order from the court that the defendant may not continue copying your work. Sometimes you may also be able to get a "preliminary injunction" to restrain further copying during the lawsuit. However, if a court grants a preliminary injunction, it will require you to post bond to cover damages suffered by the defendant during the time he is restrained if the defendant wins the underlying copyright infringement case.

A court will consider four factors in deciding whether to issue an injunction:

1. You have suffered irreparable harm;
2. Your other remedies, such as monetary damages, are inadequate to compensate you for that injury;
3. As between you and the defendant, the balance of hardships weighs in favor of protecting you; and

4.   The public interest will not be disserved by the issuance of an injunction.

While the law imposes this burden of proof on you as a plaintiff, injunctions are frequently issued in copyright infringement cases.

The decision to file a lawsuit should not be taken lightly. Simply put, litigation is not fun, and can be stressful, time-consuming, and expensive. But situations exist in which you may not have any other option but to file a lawsuit. There are a couple of basic questions you must ask before filing suit.

How do I decide whether to file suit?

Experienced copyright attorneys cannot predict whether you will prevail in a lawsuit. But they can help you assess the likelihood of your success and can help you evaluate the time and expense of litigation, your likely recovery, the damage to your reputation as a result of the infringement, and the other factors influencing your decision. Your attorney may recommend a "cease-and-desist" letter, which invites a settlement of your claim prior to filing suit.

How much does it cost to file suit?

You should discuss with your attorney her hourly rate and ask for a budget for the litigation. There may be considerable upfront costs before you even get to trial because your attorney will need to prepare a complaint and will need to prepare for and conduct discovery, including asking written questions of the defendant (interrogatories), demanding documents from the defendant, and taking depositions, as well as briefing various motions prior to trial. The court also charges a filing fee, which in the federal court for the Northern District of Illinois is at least $400.

Website Resources

Glossary

Account: A statement of monies received and/or expenses charged; the duty to account is the duty to explain the monies received by one and paid to another.

Advance: The upfront payment to an author from a publisher, based on the publisher's estimate of sales, an "advance" against expected royalties the publisher otherwise would pay as earned rather than up-front.

Allegation: A statement made by a plaintiff in his/her complaint in a lawsuit.

Assign: To transfer, as in assigning all right, title, and interest.

Assignors: The persons to whom a right or thing is transferred.

Complaint: The document written by a lawyer and filed with the court which sets forth the ways in which the plaintiff believes he or she has been wronged and the desired remedy, usually money damages.

Copyright: A statutory system of protection for works of authorship.

Copyright notice: The notice specified by statute to give notice of a claim to ownership in a copyright, most commonly: © year of publication, name of author.

Defamation: A tort (wrong) caused by making a statement which casts another in a negative light, often thought of as libel or slander.

Defendant: The party named in a lawsuit as the wrongdoer, as in the infringer in a copyright infringement lawsuit brought by a copyright owner.

Deposition: An oral interview, on the record, taken by a lawyer of a witness in a legal proceeding.

Derivative work: A work based on a previous work, such a movie based on a book or short story.

Discovery: The legal process for fact-finding prior to trial, including depositions, interrogatories, and document productions.

Fair use: A relatively small use of another's work for purposes such as comment or criticism.

False light: A tort (wrong) which exists because a person was cast in a false light which would be highly offensive to a reasonable person, an act committed with actual malice or reckless disregard for the truth.

First serialization: The first right to publish a work in a periodical.

Freelancer: A writer (or other artist) who is not an employee of a company.

Ghost writer: A writer for hire whose work will appear under the name of the person by whom he/she is being paid.

Gross profit: All of the revenues (money) received from a project less specified expenses.

Indemnity: A duty to make another whole for their loss or out-of-pocket expenses.

Independent contractor: A freelancer; not an employee.

Infringement: The act of using any of the rights of copyright without the permission of the copyright owner.

Injunction: A court order requiring a party to stop a specified activity, such as an injunction against continuing to infringe a copyright.

Interrogatories: Written questions put to a witness during discovery prior to trial.

Joint work: A work created by two authors acting together and intending to jointly own the rights in the work.

Kill fee: A fee sometimes contractually specified and payable if a commissioned article is not published.

Libel: A tort (wrong) which occurs when a false statement is made about a person and which causes injury.

Moral rights: An author's or artist's rights of attribution and integrity recognized more formally in other countries than in the United States.

Net profit: All of the revenues (money) received from a project less specified expenses.

Plaintiff: The one who starts a lawsuit by claiming that he/she has been wronged.

Prima facie: A legal term meaning "on its face."

Public domain: That which is free for anyone to use because it is no longer protected by copyright or other intellectual property law.

Public performance: The public performance of a work is the performance of it at a place open to the public or where a substantial number of persons outside of family is gathered, and includes transmission by broadcast to many places at the same time.

Reserve: Monies otherwise payable to an author held back by a publisher in case books are returned or there are other charges against an author's account.

Representation: A statement by a party to a contract that something said is true, such as a representation that "I am the sole author."

Right of privacy: Commonly thought of as the constitutional right to be left alone.

Right of publicity: The unique right of a well-known person to exploit her persona, name, likeness, and image, often set forth in state statutes.

Royalty: A periodic payment to an author based on product sales, often stated as a percentage or in cents/unit sold.

Tangible medium of expression: A concrete form from which a work can be perceived.

Tort: A wrong which is actionable at law.

Trademark: A word or symbol which designates the goods or services of a specific source and represents the goodwill associated with that source.

Warranty: A representation which is also a guarantee.

About the Authors

Mary Hutchings Reed joined the Lawyers for the Creative Arts Board in 1984, and has held every office, some of them twice! She is also honored to have received the Thomas R. Leavens Award from LCA and the Esther Rothstein Award from the Women's Bar Association of Illinois. She is a former partner in the law firms of Sidley Austin LLP and Winston & Strawn LLP, and is currently of counsel to Winston & Strawn, where she has practiced advertising, marketing, trademark, copyright, sports and entertainment law since 1989. In 2012, she was named Best Lawyers' Chicago Advertising Lawyer of the Year. Almost 20 years ago, she reduced her practice to part-time to pursue her own interests in creative writing and community service. She is the author of the leading treatise on sponsorship law, *The IEG Legal Guide to Sponsorship*; *The IEG Legal Guide to Cause Marketing*; *The Copyright Primer for Librarians and Educators*; and *LCA, The First Forty Years*.

David Creasey is an Iowa native and graduate of Grinnell College and the University of Chicago Law School. He currently practices law at Winston & Strawn LLP, where he is an associate in the litigation department. His passion for books began as small child listening for hours nightly to his mother read aloud the adventures of Johnny Orchard, Cowboy Small, Meg Murry, and countless others. Before attending law school, David taught third grade with Teach for America at Lucilia Wood Elementary School in Elaine, Arkansas, where he was able to share his love of reading and books with his students.

About the Editor

Jason Koransky is an associate in the intellectual property litigation group at Kirkland & Ellis LLP, where his practice focuses on copyright, trademark, and false advertising law. Before becoming an attorney, Jason was a journalist in the Chicago area for more than a decade, during which time his work included serving as the editor of the music magazine DownBeat.

www.ingramcontent.com/pod-product-compliance
Lightning Source LLC
Chambersburg PA
CBHW051347170526
45166CB00002B/991

* 9 7 8 1 4 9 0 9 8 1 0 2 4 *